GW01252076

Perfect Timing

poetry

Christopher Horton

tall-lighthouse

© Christopher Horton 2021

Christopher Horton has asserted his right to be identified
as the author of this work in accordance with the Copyright,
Designs & Patents Act 1988.

This book is sold subject to the condition that it shall not, by way
of trade or otherwise, be lent, resold, hired out or otherwise
circulated without the publisher's prior consent in any form
of binding or cover other than that in which it is published and
without a similar condition including this condition being imposed
on the subsequent purchaser.

Cover Design: Flora Hands, Carline Creative

A CIP record for this book is available
from the British Library

published 2021 by tall-lighthouse

ISBN 978 1 904551 10 2

tall-lighthouse
www.tall-lighthouse.co.uk

*Forget the here-and-now. We have no time
but this device of wantonness and wit.*

*Make me this present then: your hand in mine,
and we'll live out our lives in it.*

Michael Donaghy
The Present

Contents

The Homeless	1
Cabbages	2
And, yes, I have compared you to a goat	3
Rent Man's Note	4
Gastronomy	5
The Fascination	6
Members Only	7
Attila's Chair	8
Gaudi's Workshop, June 6th 1926	9
Erno Goldfinger Moves into Balfron Tower	10
The Minister as a Horse	12
Ultrasonic Mouse Deterrent	13
Red Kite at a Football Match	14
Wild Boars	15
A Wader's Perspective	16
Festival	18
Returning to the Office in the Year 2500	19
Same Air, Repeat, Same Air	21
The Crundale Buckle	22
The Valley	23
Temple	24

The Homeless

The lady who once squatted, half-cut, in the phone-box
reminds you of someone, you say.
An old friend of your family

had *comparable cheekbones, similar intonation.*
Or was it an actress from a film you watched as a girl?
Either way, you wish you could put your finger on it.

It's none of our business of course
but she sits with the freckled man
with the small head who calls us *my friends*

before asking for change.
Once, when we saw him shaking in the rain,
we gave him something to eat.

When we didn't see him the next day
we worried if he'd made the night.
We smile politely when they approach

then quicken our pace at the corner of the street.
London's like this, we tell ourselves.
Anything can become routine.

This flat on the High Street is just big enough for now.
We double-lock the door and tighten the blinds.
Lamp-posts project the scene where they sleep.

We try not to talk about them.
As the months grow colder, we talk about them more.
We don't want to know their names.

Cabbages

As often retold, my grandfather stood on a battered frigate
two days after D-Day. Food was scarce
(they'd forgotten to load half the supplies).
As captain of the vessel he ordered they drop a tender
barely sixty yards from shore. This was Normandy, near Juno.
The Germans, their lines now broken, were lying low.

From the signal deck, my grandfather
had sighted a small farmhouse, surrounded
by thousands of Danish Ballheads, fully grown,
just out of season but still with emerald skins.
On account of his schoolboy French, he went alone
to ask the farmer if he might take some for his famished crew.
Donnez-moi quelques choux, s'il vous plaît.
Jusqu'au fin de la guerre, nous aimons vos choux beaucoup.
The farmer hugged him like a brother,
then filled his outstretched arms
with half a dozen of the biggest he could find.
Back on board, the men applauded the returning hero.
Nothing wasted, each cabbage was boiled down to make a soup.

Other stories came less easily, or never came.
No one asked about the last Arctic convoy to Murmansk
from which only half the men returned.
Sometimes, you could sense a specific kind of silence,
when his hands trembled just slightly
then steadied to a grasp as he fought
to stop more memories from pouring in.

And, yes, I have compared you to a goat

but not a goat that bucks and froths,
who, in the fable at least, is tethered
to a post by the village green.

No, more a goat, that in the liberal scope
of a paddock or low-lying meadow,
knows and tastes a kind of freedom,

who might think to roam from here
were it not for the nutrition of wildflower,
or the plenitude of grass, or the subtlety

of dew as it descends in the early hours
so that each blade bows with weight
of little more than a single, unbroken drop.

Rent Man's Note

Yes, I have missed you, Ms Maud,
on that monthly round from Pitfield Street
to Hemsworth Street in N1 gloom.
I have even missed your yard's assorted junk:
a punctured chair, shards of mirror-glass,
the crooked plastic *Number Six* mounted,
lop-sided, on your pock marked door.

You will remember me, Ms Maud,
as a pale and dumb-faced inquisitor,
a dog-eared sheet of names clinched
to a flimsy clipboard, held in sweaty palms,
and you will know me as the young man
who asked you why you hadn't paid the rent.

Do not think I cared for it, Ms Maud –
this unenviable duty passed on to me
of waiting in the cold for you,
in nylon shirt and mismatched tie,
the giving testimony to the breach of clauses
that never seemed to find full stops,
or that I prepared the papers *eagerly* for court,
or wanted the judge
to call your name and mine.

Gastronomy

Take the last lobster and put it in a tank,
put the tank in a cute little restaurant
in Saint-Malo, have a curvaceous waitress
buzzing around a seated couple. Picture the man
in that couple, a stout and tight-faced middle-aged gent –
a line of spittle cascading his chin, pooling
to souse the croutons that float in a thick fish soup.
His younger wife, or mistress, is tackling a gigantic plate
of steaming *moules marinières* as her entrée.

The music is Édith Piaf's *Non, je ne regrette rien*.
The lobster has grown to endure Édith Piaf
but would much prefer Monique Serf.
The sea, as seen through the window, is cutting
into the frame. No, scratch that. The sea is going out
on a whim. There is a picture of a lobster on the wall,
depicted, not in a tank but gripped by a rockpool.
The lobster in the tank stares at the picture for recognition.
The lobster in the picture clearly can't stare back.
The lobster in the tank does not know this
and assumes that the lobster in the picture is stuck-up.

Now, the (real) lobster catches sight of the wife, or mistress,
and his antennae flinch (a sure sign of a lobster's interest).
The lobster in the tank is infatuated
by her pale powdered skin, her pearl lipstick,
the way she prises open the steadfast lip
of the last locked shell. The lobster in the tank
would like to know more about this woman.
The middle-aged man calls to the waitress,
runs his fat finger down the menu,
then looks at his wife, or mistress,
before finally plumping for the lobster.

The Fascination

Please, one more time, tell me that story:
a pub on the corner of a barely lit road
in a town long since left to chimera

a soon-to-be couple talking postgraduate,
a fire kindling in the snug – at least allow
a glow, a flush of heat to glister

their well-matched cheeks, his eyes tracing
the outline of her unfathomable hair,
and her eyes beckoning. If not this,

bring to sense the force of their fascination,
what followed when speech failed them
and they needed to head back to the halls?

Surely, at the juncture between the said
and unsaid, it was not just any planet or star
that cleared Orion's Belt but Mars, given away

by its iron pelt, rising above the last tree
in the park. Was it then, as if a sign had been given,
that he felt a button in his coat pocket

and felt it burn deep to the pit of his palm
or, later, at the bus stop, when he saw in her eyes
a whole universe, or the possibility of one,

seeming closer in that moment
but still a place he knew he would never know
and that was everything to know.

Members Only

> *In 2007, a social networking group was set up for those who like to sit at the front of driverless Dockland Light Railway trains and pretend they're driving. It had over one-thousand-four hundred members.*

Watch them as they nod to each other
discreetly, like Freemasons entering a lodge,
as they move to their usual positions,
place their hands on their knees.

See how their fingers twitch as it first pulls away,
when the drawn-up whir moves up the spine.
In their minds they are the real drivers
of these driverless trains. In their minds

they're in total control when the city opens up
and every part of the track reveals itself
a system of parts, switching points, expansion joints,
cables, pandrol clips, lag crews.

At night, they dream with their eyes open.
It's the flutter of a pulse,
the dilation of their pupils, the tremor
of a stray nerve, that tells their loved ones

the journey's about to start. Watch carefully
and time the pauses at the end of each breath.
You could trace the stations as they near the end of the line.
Westferry, Limehouse, Shadwell, Bank.

Attila's Chair

Of all those who ventured
to the island of Torcello
(walked down the narrow path,
past the wooden footbridge,
the old farm house, some nodding hens)
to sit on Attila's Chair –
believing that by doing so they would,
as folklore has it, wed within a year –
how many felt a hand in theirs as they touched
the chair's worn and pitted surface,
tapped their feet against its solid base,
pressed their calves together like children
waiting for something to happen?

And how many in some quiet moment since –
taken from a life of conjugal bickering,
or stymied ambition, or singlehood,
or in the short breath between
the *I* and *do* — recalled what it was
that first brought them here,
or the time of day, the tint and texture
of the light, the journey back by boat
across the pale green lagoon?

Gaudi's Workshop, June 6th 1926

> *'Gaudi was walking uncertainly and distractedly in the street that afternoon on 7th June, 1926...'*
> Gaudi: The Life of a Visionary, J. Castellar-Gasso

Gaudi's lunch, wrapped in hessian,
hangs delicately on a piece of string
(chorizo, cheese, tomato bread).
It is kept here to avoid getting in the way.

Order is important, or at least there's a system.
There is, too, the aroma of drying Indian ink,
and the stifling taste of plaster dust.

An alabaster lantern, barely lit,
illuminates a large drawing-board.
Sketches of La Sagrada Familia are pinned to it.

The towers are shown as complete.
One is inked, the others remain in pencil.
They might be symmetrical.

Outside, a eucalyptus tree stands
in the courtyard, leaning in towards the window.
Its shadow, traced against brickwork
distorts its shape and size.

In a week's time, a group of mourners
will walk from the heart of Barcelona,
slowly, in procession, heads bowed,
not stopping to look inside this room.

Tomorrow he'll be hit by a tram.
He won't be recognised at first.
In his pocket they'll find a small
crumpled bible, flecked with Indian ink.

Erno Goldfinger Moves into Balfron Tower

'I want to experience, at first hand, the size of the rooms...'
Erno Goldfinger, who lived with his wife Ursula in
Balfron Tower for two months from February 1968

What goes, Erno? I'm looking right back at you,
                out across the graticule of junctions and up,
    up to where surely you still stand on a pulpit balcony,

gimlet-eyed, dressed in a ushanka
                      and bespoke suit – English cut.
            The morning light kicks in and in a blink

this becomes the first day of your experiment
                for elevated living, Flat 130, 26th floor.
                  Inside, your books vie for shelf space

like siblings, each one outdating the next,
                their spines wrinkled and flexed,
            years after the rush of a first reading.

Whose theory on form and function inspires you most, Erno?
        When Le Corbusier leaves you cold, do you turn
                to Adolf Loos or dear Walter Gropius?

And tonight, when you pour Russian champagne
        into your new neighbours' glasses will you look them
                in the eyes and promise a new world?

The room behind you lies like an idea,
              adjusts to its precise proportions, its tailored line.
     The light switches in the doorframes are revolutionary!

How elegantly Ursula walks the corridors, holds the flats
           of her hands against the newly painted walls,
    takes the scent of each lick as if inhaling magnolia.

The Minister as a Horse

No one can quite remember whether it was
during the Select Committee or in a Cabinet meeting
that he first whinnied, then flared his nostrils
at the Secretary for Culture, Media and Sport.
Certainly this wasn't minuted and either way
such things are often overlooked in Whitehall.

You might have thought the formal opposition
would have raised an objection
when, before a cross-party vote,
he bolted through the central lobby and headed out
towards St James's Park to chew the cud;
or that a conscientious constituent would have written
to express deep concern when, at the opening of a hospital,
he tried to eat the ribbon.

But this is not what transpired. Miraculously,
he survived the reshuffle, proudly strutting out
of Number Ten in newly fitted hooves.
Only after he had been put out to graze
in *The Other Place*, did someone enquire
as to whether, in polite society such as this,
it was really the done thing to toss one's mane.

Ultrasonic Mouse Deterrent

Listen, the mice are behind the skirting boards again
apparently immune to the special plugs we bought.
At least we lie above the pitch of ultrasonic screams
now riding the fug of left-out dhansak. Those rodents
are playing us for fools, making-out in the nooks,
tutoring their offspring on the strengths and weaknesses
of cereal packets, the entrances and exits of kitchen units,
the niche architecture of breadbins.

Tell me, why is so much of this amplified?
The window's reflection frames us.
My arm rests on your hips. We're simulating
the small movements of sleep, but both of us are pit-eyed,
staring at the curvature of furniture, none of it matching,
each piece a cut from our lives.

We don't know in this dirty light whether it's morning
or night. Or if the mice know we're here, cogitating,
while our bodies throb to the same age old beat
and are as warm as theirs.

Red Kite at a Football Match

Where the Beechdean Stand faced across the Chiltern Hills
and a line of trees waved in a chilled wind,
my father and I were seeing out a likely nil nil draw,
or at least the players were, when at the centre circle
a high elbow led to a sudden aggravated huddle
(no more, in reality, than a pantomime scuffle).
Nothing much would come of it save a straight red
and the crowd kept on baying as the carded player walked.
I looked around to my father for a reaction or at least
a shared grumble of sorts so near to the end of the half
but he seemed somewhere else far away. It was the red kite
that had him attentively looking to the heavens
as it angled its wings against the air so as to be carried
by an uplift before dropping to the seam of the chalk siding,
then onto the villages set against the other side of the valley.
And on the way home, it was not the last-minute winner
that we spoke of but that bird, its perfect timing,
its expert mediation of the steady thermal current
through the slanting of its wings and rudder-tilting of its tail.

Here, now, the game fades to irrelevance among other games
but the moment of flight comes back to me more clearly.
In the snapshot, my father is focussed with his head up,
(clutching his flask of lukewarm tea, scarf wrapped to his chin)
and I'm only watching him, not the football pitch
nor, any longer, that red kite as it leaves us still in that stand.

Wild Boars

What we come to believe is what we want to believe
when the streets are paused to a standstill,
the surrounding hills our only retreat. For me,
the snapping of beech, the stirring of foliage,
was more real than the light that shone,
late afternoon, across from Marriage Wood.

When the two of them ran, we thought they were dogs –
at first – from the sound of their movement alone.
How quickly they made their way, one behind the other,
a maverick convoy of muscle and flesh
passing steadfastly to a destination only they knew.

Through the cover of branches, nothing was certain.
I could swear there was the lowering of bird song
and the sudden glint of an eye as they gathered pace,
surging uphill where no way seemed possible.

Still at that point of half-believing they were dogs,
we waited patiently for their owner walking behind,
for a call at least. In the moments afterwards, the birds
regained their confidence but no voice was heard.

A Wader's Perspective

Three months into the first lockdown, the house was alive
with a plethora of screens, appliances and gizmos.
Their feral warmth emanated
from where we kept them charging
like beasts tethered to a trough
and over to where we sat, still caught up
in fears too bleak to share in the chat rooms and platforms
or to utter to our loved ones before a tide
of Zoom and Teams, bulletins and smart-phone ephemera.

Outside, foxes were everywhere.
We watched them from the upstairs window
trotting down the street at midday,
proud citizens of a new world.
We heard them fooling around by the bins,
stumbling over pizza boxes and wine bottles.
Their joyous screams kept us up
and so did the owl with its ostinato soundtrack
delivered from a sniper's perch or mic spot.
Either way, we never located it by tree,
not before its regular slot,
or second-guessed which way its turntable-head faced
in the gap between our lawn and the railway tracks.

And then, all at once, without so much
as a re-induction course or manual step-guide
being poked through our letterbox,
we were outside again,
released to the ghosted roads and finally the River Adur,
to be toe-ended into a sanitised kayak
and make our way down current
where everything seemed vivid and fat with neglect.

Neither purely tidal nor typical estuary,
the high water carried us
as a sea trout jumped the top eye of a fisherman's rod
and swam off unencumbered.
A wader came down from the bank, carefully stepping out
with its ludicrous green pins, its elongated beak.
There by the side of the reed bed our senses engaged it,
and there, too, it stared and stared at us
and was, in every way, amazed by us.

Festival

On the case of the missing wood from Johnson's farm,
the parish had made its verdict
well before festival day
when some local sons attacked two *travellers*
and left them bloodied on the patch of couch grass,
beside their trailer home.

We saw the rest on local news,
pre-recorded, from inside A&E,
camera close-ups of every bruise, an interview
with a lad of nine about what had taken place,
an angled shot of his father's swollen face.

It was an age before the police took note.
When they did, they spoke in tongues.
No fingerprints, no leads, no fuss, no bother,
a general rule of thumb.
Gypsies, they said. *Ah! We know*, they said.
Apparently, some sort of deal was done.

All too soon, the townspeople moved on.
Same as every year, they took down the bunting,
scrubbed the war-memorial,
tended to its pots and beds. The float-procession
was what most chose to talk about.

The pubs were brimming. Flags were still out.
It was the same hot summer I saved for my first radio,
Yugoslavia finally broke and England lost
to Germany on penalties. I remember that.

Returning to the Office in the Year 2500

They enter the Human Resources Department
just as it was left. It's the antiquities research team
that first files in, decked-out
in regulation space suits.

All they can hear is the crackle
then cutting-up of radio transmission,
slow breathing amplified
within their steamed-up helmets.

The photocopier is labelled *Out of Order*.
The shredder was detached mid-shred.
A bundle of A4 paper has yellowed
like all those manuscripts left by the ancients.

If they were to load the paper,
the printer shelf would fall apart
in their heavy hands, its rusty springs
landing on a top-surface of mites and motes.

They wouldn't know how to load it anyway.
Paper is no longer a thing.
The football mug on Brian's name-tagged desk
has fungi growing out of it.

The piece will now be assigned
to the Museum of The Distant Past,
where it can be kept in the rare mug section.
It is of archaeological interest.

They scan the curious motif
of a team called Lincoln City.
Football no longer exists,
neither do mugs. Tea is still a thing.

In the stationery cupboard,
a line of staplers and hole punchers
sit aligned on the shelf,
suggesting these were valuable tools.

The office system is perfectly preserved.
There can be no confusion
when finding the folders and laminates.
Almost everything denotes a culture

of mundane endeavour and routine
but, fleetingly, fun may have occurred.
Above the cupboard door,
someone wrote *Brian4Sarah*.

This passed for humour once.
The specialist team take a photo
to age-test back at the lab
then wheel the most significant findings

through the reception area,
onto the empty parking lot,
finally giving the demolition team
the all clear.

Same Air, Repeat, Same Air
after the first Lockdown, 2020

Side step away from the lads at the bus stop
as they emit thick plumes of white vapour
that surge towards the edge of the troposphere.
Dread to breathe the same air as the young
who may or may not recover
from stories of party *conquests*,
so clearly made up that their lies cause ripples
of laughter, then outright chuckles,
from the tidy wives of Bromley.
But they, and we, are scared, mostly.
We do not laugh too hard for fear
that we might breathe too much of the same air.

Breathe out, get on the bus, mask up.

At Bickley, a lady in a worn care-home uniform
gets on the bus, tired from her shift,
an outdated medical-style watch hung
precariously from her top pocket,
her ID badge displaying a smile
now absent from her real-life face.
People shuffle away from her onto different seats,
stare at her with mild admiration but also fear.

The bus stops, empties, masks are removed.
We head towards the market,
our mouths feeding the air,
the air feeding us, but we are happy to be out of the bus
and each passenger sends out a silent prayer.
Impossible now to remember how things used to be
and what we thought we knew before.
By which I mean, before we really understood
that all things are connected,
that we all share the same air.

The Crundale Buckle

All night Storm Bella blew through our new home,
enacting its seventy-miles-an-hour stress test
of our rafters, our collar beams and finely-weighted joists.
You felt every rattle and hardly slept a wink.

Next day, avoiding Bella's wake (a tree split in half
on Olantigh Road), we hiked two well-matched escarpments
at Crundale. These we remade as whale ribs washed-up
on the sandy shores of distant archipelagos. Fully puffed,

we took to our viewing point, looked down a line
to where the woods had been cut to fields and tracks,
close to where a gilt-bossed buckle was once found,
no other treasures, just this, an Anglo-Saxon fastener

depicting a golden fish and a snake biting its own tail.
Now nestled in the British Museum, the buckle seems unique
but what other possible *finds* still lay buried beneath us
as we descended the steep incline that led to Sole Street?

All things must return to the surface. Trust this adage
and trust that the traces of those generations before ours,
crushed down, layered into the body of the hill, will re-emerge
to air, sun-proud, pushed back up by its chalky scales.

The Valley

This valley is beside itself, but there is nothing left
for the sky to give now the day's last measure of rainfall
has been released, leaving its cover of cloud emptied out,
hightailing across the far weald, bereft of contraband.

In the small coppice by the muddy track, pheasants tread
then trip repeatedly so that the sound of breaking twigs,
as they clumsily make their way through the undergrowth,
becomes at one with the fragile cacophony of my wired heart.

The volume turns up a notch with so much on the line
between two continents. All winter, messages from your family
have trilled into your inbox and something pulls you back,
that part of you that transcends the tightening lockdown.

When you catch me here, still thinking about the pheasants –
flushed bouquets of pheasants with eager, hungry eyes –
you tell me instead about the kakapo, its striking plumage,
its homing instinct and distinctive nesting habits.

We will take this last cold snap upon us and hold inside
the *other* bird that never rests, the one we know too well.

Temple

We sit here looking down to the temple.
Beyond it, the sea carries on, as it always has.
Only today we're the ones feeling timeless,
having come through so much, having made it here.

I would go into this but it hardly matters now,
besides all things have come together.
Truly, I sense we've found a kind of peace
or at least the same cure that's held within

the fresh morning air, the overlay of birdsong.
All of which brings me back to what we came here for.
First, tell me again that love will always win out
and I will tell you about those people before us

who, having walked for weeks with all they could carry,
came to this place so that, at a specific time of year
and a specific time of day, they could observe
a single beam of light enter into the main temple room
through no more than an aperture in the rock

which then, along a central axis, refracted
onto the far inner wall across from where they sat.
And I will tell you too, how once this was seen,
once that witnessing had passed into them,
they would start the long journey back home again.

Acknowledgements & Thanks

Thanks to the editors of *Poetry London, Fuselit, The Wolf, Poetry Wales, City State: New London Poetry (Penned in the Margins), Days of Roses Anthology (1)* and *City Lighthouse Poetry Anthology (tall-lighthouse)*.

The Minister as a Horse was commended in the National Poetry Competition.

Ultrasonic Mouse Deterrent was highly commended in the Bridport Prize.

Wild Boars won the South Downs Poetry Festival Competition and *The Crundale Buckle* was highly commended in the same year of the competition.

Special thanks to Declan Ryan, Simon Barraclough, James Byrne, Jon Stone and James Mason.

Most of all, I would like to acknowledge the support of my parents, friends and fiancée.